Dear Husband
A Good Wife's Heart for Her Husband

Rachel Renée

KNIGHTDALE, NORTH CAROLINA

Copyright © 2016 by **Rachel Renée Smith**

All rights reserved. No part of this publication may be reproduced, distributed or transmitted in any form or by any means, without prior written permission.

Rachel Renée /Rain Publishing
PO Box 702
Knightdale, NC 27545
www.RainPublishing.com

Dear Husband/ Rachel Renée. -- 1st ed.
ISBN 978-0-9977748-1-8

Reviews for Dear Husband

"Relevant... Compelling... Transparent. These words don't quite describe the feeling I've experienced reading *Dear Husband*. Rachel Renee has written a masterpiece that is profound in truth, and rooted in absolute grace. This book is both convicting and liberating at the same time. She has embodied the ideology and the words that every husband longs to hear and experience.

The honesty and depth from which she writes is paramount and refreshing. The way that she corrects the reader without cutting the reader is brilliant. This book will undoubtedly lead to breakthrough and change for marriages and future marriages. *Dear Husband* is not just a book that you read, but it's a feeling and emotion that should be experienced. Kudos to Rachel Renee for writing a book that will speak for ages to come."

~David Burrus, Relationship Expert, Author of *The Blueprint*

"*Dear Husband* is a wife's declaration of love to her husband and a celebration of God's gift of covenant marriage. In this book Rachel Renee uncovers the power of submission, shines a light on intimacy, opens the lines of communication between spouses and through declarations holds both husbands and wives accountable for the success of their union. This book is a tool that will bring deliverance to couples everywhere."

~Calvin Holland and Linda Dominique Grosvenor-Holland, Love Better Institute

"*Dear Husband* is helpful for those who are married or preparing for marriage. Singles can use this book to help free themselves from behavior that goes along with being single. The letters are very informative, very clear, and I'm glad it is what it is – your heart, your experience, an authentic space, a maturely written piece that exemplifies the heart of God."

~Marcel Anderson, Accelerating Men, Inc.

"Rachel Renee truly captured God's heart for His married daughters with *Dear Husband: A Good Wife's Heart for Her Husband*. Those who love The Holy Scriptures will find the Spirit deeply embedded in these words, and will have their faith built up to persevere through seasons of learning. I highly value writings that honor God's will for high-stakes relationships and conclude this work to be…priceless."

~Zari Banks, M.Ed.

www.ZariBanks.co

"*Dear Husband* is not only for married couples but it can also be a tool to assist singles on their journey to married life.

You can 'hear the heart' of Rachel Renee as she shares her wisdom about what it means to be a good wife and how husbands can help in the process. Excellent read!"

~Shamine Marie McDowell, Author of *My Journey from Perverseness to Purity*

*These letters are written to my future husband,
the Man I can trust with my heart.*

CONTENTS

You Can Trust Me 1
I Am Not Your Enemy 2
I Have Feelings Too 5
Let's Commit To: 6
Let's Talk About It 9
Respect 10
Let's Commit To: 12
I Need You Sexually 15
Let's Commit To: 18
Romance without Finance? 21
Let's Commit To: 23
We are One 25
What We Do and Who We Do It With 26
Let's Commit To: 30
I'm Trusting You With My Life 35
Accountability and Development 36
Your Submission to God 37
Let's Commit To: 38

Dear Husbands 41
Dear Wives 43
To My Husband.. 45
More Resources 46
About the Author.. 47

Introduction

Dear Husbands, I wrote these letters for my future husband and I am sharing them with you as a wife who submitted to the process of becoming a committed and faithful woman with a heart that is turned toward her husband. Through many tests, God has preserved my heart and my desire to be a good wife as well as to empower other wives to continue praying and believing God's best for their marriages.

I published this book for two main purposes: (1) to help husbands understand their wives' hearts for them and (2) to lend my voice in support of good wives who truly desire to grow with their husbands in a great marriage.

My prayer is that by transparently sharing my heart, it will help you to see your wife's heart. Sometimes the pressures and circumstances we deal with in life cause us to have an inherent distrust of the people closest to us, even while perfect strangers receive the benefit of the doubt. The truth is that good wives want their husbands to win in life. Good wives love unconditionally. Good wives want you to grow together. If you see your wife within the pages of this book, know that you have a good one.

Dear Husbands, I pray that you will not ignore the call to love your wife with your heart, and in your words, thoughts, and actions.

I believe that true love can exist between a man and a woman, and I believe in the institution of marriage. Therefore, I am sharing these letters and baring my soul in support of good wives everywhere who just want to love their men and fulfill God's purpose for their marriages.

Love and Blessings,

Rachel Renee

Dear Husband,

YOU CAN TRUST ME

I love you and I am completely sold out for you so I would like you to understand that you don't have to fear rejection from me. You can share your heart with me completely and I will not abuse it. I am so honored that God trusts me with your heart and I know it is a great and precious responsibility. Even before we got married, I prayed that God would guard your heart because I know how hard it can be to trust someone when you've been hurt or betrayed before. If there are any areas where you are hurting and still in need of healing, I am committed to helping you walk through those things. I am a firm believer in us having a great life together, better than our lives ever were before because we now have each other. You are safe with me. Please help me to understand how to best support you when you are having a challenging day or dealing with difficult feelings so I can give you the support that you want and need.

I Am Not Your Enemy

I really don't know any other way to say this. I am not your enemy. I am always on your side, even when we disagree. I am always on your team. This means you don't have to be defensive with me when we don't see things the same way. I may think your viewpoint is wrong but that doesn't diminish my opinion of you and it definitely doesn't change my respect for you.

> **I am always on your side.**

When I ask questions I am either trying to understand your point of view or challenge you to think about it differently. This is all part of my role in helping you with your purpose. I am an extra set of eyes for you. I am an extra pair of hands for you. I am an extra pair of ears for you. Do you see what I mean? When I hear and see things differently than you, you are receiving the benefit of another perspective to help you plan and strategize. Your vision can be more complete because you have access to new angles and vantage points through me. I'm here for your advancement, never to tear you down. There is never competition between us because everything that is in me is for you. This way our partnership brings the most glory to God.

> **Everything that is in me is for you.**

I want to collaborate with you to come up with solutions. Please don't receive my feedback as me taking shots at you. If my communication has been abrasive in the past, I apologize. Please gently point that out to me so that I can correct it.

I love you so I am making a very conscious effort to approach you as peacefully as possible when there is an issue. If I am truly angry or frustrated I will even wait until I calm down before I approach you so that I can keep my tone at a peaceful level.

I pray and ask God to lead me and guide me when talking with you so that I can approach you in the right way, at the right time. Would you please be open to my communication? A defensive wall is really not necessary when it comes to me – it would actually serve us more harm than good because it prevents us from interacting with each other in an intimate space where we really see each other and communicate from a place of total authenticity.

I trust you and I am totally open to you. I want you to see into me because I believe that you love me, even with all my flaws. With all my heart I hope you know that I am never, at any time, your enemy. There is not a moment of the day that I want to see you suffer. There is not even the slightest desire in me to personally be the source of your pain. I want to always bring love, healing, and even comfort to your life.

This means that you can make mistakes and I still won't be against you. This means I can point out an area where we can improve together but it doesn't mean I am angry or disappointed in you. You are allowed to be human in front of me. I knew when I met you that you weren't perfect. I am far from perfect myself so how can I hold you to that standard? I knew we wouldn't always agree. I knew there would be days when you would work my last nerve, and vice versa. None of that outweighs my love for you.

I Have Feelings Too

I am human as well so I need some room to make mistakes without you holding a grudge against me. I am not going to have the perfect tone of voice every time. I am not going to choose the exact right combination of words every time. I have challenging days and weird moods every once in a while. I am asking you for grace. I'm asking you to see past my flaws in those moments and *trust my heart*. I may not be totally loving at all times, but my heart is still for you. If you give me a chance, I will fix it because as I said, I don't want to be a source of pain for you. If there is anything that I am doing on a consistent basis that really bothers you and rubs you the wrong way, please talk to me about it and give me the opportunity to correct it. It is not my desire to continue any behavior that upsets you or makes you uncomfortable.

The bottom line is, I love you and I am always for you. Believe that.

Let's Commit To:

1. Ask questions to find understanding BEFORE getting angry, believing the best of each other unless proven otherwise.

2. Pray for wisdom before communicating with each other if it is a sore spot or if one or both of us is upset.

3. Seek counseling for issues we can't seem to resolve between us.

Notes:

8 · RACHEL RENEE

Dear Husband,

LET'S TALK ABOUT IT

We are building something great together and as with any team who is creating something worth building, we need to be able to communicate effectively with each other. Let's not allow our lives to get so busy that we can't even have a conversation.

It can be so easy to get engrossed in our work and our daily routines and before we know it, have no clue what is going on in each other's worlds. I don't ever want us to stop sharing dreams, visions, and the cuts and scrapes we collect along the way. Can we be vulnerable with each other? Before you were anything else, you were my friend, someone I could share anything with and know that I was in a safe place. I love hearing your heart about any and everything and I pray that nothing ever gets in the way of that.

> **Let's not be too busy to talk.**

I see the way you communicate with the people you lead and serve and I am so impressed. You are accountable for your actions and you hold your team members accountable as well. You have excellent planning and leadership skills. I appreciate that you use your leadership skills to benefit our household. I enjoy receiving feedback from you when I am doing a great job. Please also tell me what you need from me so that I can be a better support to you.

Respect

It is very important to me that our home be a peaceful safe haven for our family; that's why I work so hard to keep a peaceful tone when I communicate with you. Undoubtedly we will have tense moments and I hope we can always strive to speak to each other with love and kindness. If you raise your voice at me it can be intimidating or even frightening and send the message that you don't really care about my feelings. It would also make me feel like there is a lack of respect if you yell at me as you would a child. For you to speak harshly toward me in front of anyone else would signal an even deeper level of disrespect.

> **Yelling in anger is disrespectful and damages trust.**

If you ever have the desire to speak to me in those ways, can you try to avoid it if at all possible? While they may just seem like words, when hurled out in anger, it feels like violence to me. It damages trust and my sense of security with you. It transforms you from my protector to someone I feel I need to be protected from.

If you feel that level of anger and want to direct it toward me, would you please pray or seek wise counsel first? Try to understand what happened to cause you to harbor anger and resentment toward me. Let's please talk about it and straighten it out. If I have done anything that angered you or hurt your feelings in any way, let's resolve it so that we can move forward together.

Let's Commit To:

1. Talk through conflict in gentle, respectful tones, understanding that love is our foundation so we can conquer anything else together.

2. Schedule time in our calendars to talk about our household and our relationship so we can keep each other in the loop and make sure we are on track for our goals.

3. Check in with each other every day to stay connected and to just express love and support.

4. To only discuss marital issues with people we both approve who are committed to supporting our marriage, not just to helping one of us.

Notes:

Dear Husband,

I NEED YOU SEXUALLY

I don't hear this talked about enough, but women have a real need and desire for sex, just as men do. I have been in so many marriage seminars where women were characterized as often avoiding sex while men couldn't get enough of it. That's just not accurate concerning all relationships.

How can I say this? I want you. I need you. My love for you makes me crave you to the point where it drives me crazy. I can actually start to trip over something so simple like how you look when you are working on a project, worshipping God, or speaking to an audience, how your body looks in your business attire, your smile, how your lips move when you talk, how your voice sounds on the phone, or really how you do anything that you do…

> **Sex is important to the success of our marriage.**

When things are good with us there probably isn't much I wouldn't do to make you feel good. I like being able to help you relax and take the edge off your day. Besides that, I feel such a bond between us when we connect physically. This is something that cannot be duplicated anywhere. It is spiritual. When we are together it is as if no one else exists but us and I could stay in that place with you forever.

I think it's important for you to understand that if I am avoiding sex I could genuinely be exhausted or not feeling well or it could be due to some issues that we need to deal with. Perhaps I can use more help around the house or something unrelated is upsetting me.

When things aren't good with us I may not be so ready to jump into the bed with you. For you to enter such an intimate space, please realize the level of trust that we share. If you have been ignoring me, or not speaking nicely to me, or if you rarely compliment me or make me feel special, it's like my body develops trust issues and doesn't want to let you in. Try speaking to me kindly and touching me affectionately.

If you have been attentive to me and things are seemingly good but I am not willing, can we talk about why? Let's get counseling if we are having an ongoing issue in this area. Maybe something more serious is going on. If you can be patient with me and try to help me identify the problem, it could be rewarding for both of us.

> **Affectionate words and touch help.**

I understand that stereotypes don't really help us so I can't assume that you always want sex either. You work hard and I am sure there are times you may not feel up to the task and I can be patient with that. If there is an ongoing pattern of you not wanting it though, that indicates there is an issue that we need to discuss and perhaps get help with.

We may not always want sex but it is of crucial importance to our marriage that we do it. I think of it as part of the glue that holds us together. Let's commit to doing whatever it takes to keep our marriage healthy, which includes regular physical intimacy. With your love and support I am confident that we can work through any barriers and enjoy each other the way we were created to.

Let's Commit To:

1. **Agree on a range or minimum of how many times per week/month we will have sex.**

2. **Talk about what turns us on.**

3. **Talk about what turns us off.**

4. Talk about things that get in the way of our intimacy.

5. Get help when we can't resolve intimacy issues on our own.

Notes:

Dear Husband,

ROMANCE WITHOUT FINANCE?

If there is anything that can potentially put a damper on our sex life, it is lack of finances. Being broke isn't exactly the sexiest thing in the world, but personally, if we are praying through difficult situations together for our breakthrough that can be a tremendous turn-on for me. I digress.

In all seriousness, mismanagement and deception where it regards finances will kill our marriage, literally. A family needs stability: a roof, food, clothing, utilities – all those things are important. God promised to provide everything we need but we can't blame Him for our mismanagement of what He gives us.

I need to know that I can trust you to make sound financial decisions for our household. I need to know you are communicating and consulting with me about financial matters so that I am not in the dark about what is going on. We should be purposefully working together to manage our finances so that we are not working against each other by default.

> **We should purposefully work together to manage our finances.**

It's important to me that we are not racking up debt, that we can provide for not only basic necessities but have fun together as a family, that we give a minimum of ten percent of our income to the ministries that spiritually feed us plus gifts/offerings, and that we create an emergency fund as well as long-term savings.

Let's Commit To:

1. Discuss and write down our financial goals for our family.

2. Be transparent with each other about money issues.

3. Cut out unnecessary spending.

4. Continually seek education about how to make the best financial decisions.

5. Get professional services to help us manage at every level of our success.

Notes:

Dear Husband,

WE ARE ONE

Being married means that we are no longer two people, we have merged and become one. What was once you is me, what was once me is you and now it is, We. This is something that we must fiercely protect because there are so many people and things that if given the opportunity could drive a wedge in between us and break our bond.

Boundaries are needed from the beginning to hedge us in and protect our marriage, otherwise, we could find ourselves in a gradual progression toward certain destruction. We must ensure that we regard our relationships in the proper order:

1. God First
2. Each Other
3. Our Children (if any)
4. Everyone Else Who Matters

There should be no negotiation on this. If we base our decisions on this order of importance, we can't go wrong. With God first, we should be seeking Him daily concerning our family and making decisions that please Him, which should really take care of everyone else. When we seek God concerning our marriage, He shows us how to love and care for each other so that we are properly covered, and the same thing with our children.

What We Do and Who We Do It With

When we esteem our marriage relationship above relationships with other people, we can keep people away from us who can potentially harm our marriage. If we are putting each other first after God, we won't be tempted to prioritize anyone else which would be dangerous. Elevating friends and family members over spouses creates resentment and drama that we don't want.

Since we are one in marriage, it is important to realize that whatever we do, we are involving each other. What affects you affects me. If you are lying, cheating, and stealing, then I'm guilty of the same by association because we are one entity, and vice-versa. We are one and I care about how we are represented in the world. I took your last name and I want it to always be a name that I am proud of. Likewise, I want to always carry myself in a way that honors you as my husband.

> If you are lying, cheating, and stealing, then I'm guilty of the same by association because we are one entity.

Neglecting to place the proper boundaries around our marriage can lead to inappropriate relationships with other people. Regular flirting and spending time with someone you are attracted to outside our marriage can lead to a physical relationship, all of which is cheating and will kill our marriage. For me, emotional and physical affairs are the highest level of betrayal in marriage. I don't want this for us. Engaging in sex with someone outside of our marriage is a major violation. If this happened it would be like you forced me to be intimate with a third party without my consent while also endangering my health.

The thing about affairs is that they can start out so innocently. It can easily start with a friend that you spend too much time talking to, then getting personal with in conversation, then perhaps venting to them about marital issues and spending time with them on a regular basis.

In marriage, sharing the responsibilities of life can sometimes become stressful and frustrating, which suddenly makes other relationships look so much more inviting and fun. Let's not fall into this trap and maintain balance in our relationship.

Let's safeguard our marriage by making sure that all opposite sex friends are mutual friends who support our commitment. Let's be open and honest with each other when a friend or acquaintance crosses the line and disrespects our marriage in any way.

> **Our friends must be mutual friends who support our commitment to each other.**

This may be unpleasant, but let's also be honest enough to tell each other if we feel challenged or tempted to do things that are not good for us, whether it is being attracted to someone outside the marriage, being tempted to abuse drugs or other substances, or being tempted to engage in any negative activities. Be honest with yourself so that you can be honest with me. Let's rely on our strength as a couple and our relationship with God to keep us from falling.

Let's Commit To:

1. Respect each other with our thoughts, words, and actions.

2. Hold ourselves to the highest moral and ethical standards as we represent each other.

3. Strive to be trustworthy people with each other and with those we interact with in our lives.

4. Put God first, each other second, and our children third with everyone else following behind this order of importance in our lives.

5. Test our words and actions against this: <u>if you have to hide it, you shouldn't do it</u> (unless we are talking about fun gifts and surprises).

6. Be honest with each other if we are tempted to do something that could hurt ourselves or our

marriage so we can work through it and/or get help.

7. Ensure that our friends are mutual friends.

Notes:

Dear Husband · 33

Dear Husband,

I'M TRUSTING YOU WITH MY LIFE

I believe that you are the head of our family, so I agree to submit to you as my leader. This does not mean that I am incapable of leading, it means that by marrying you, I am literally choosing to submit to your leadership and trust you with my life. You took on the responsibility of caring and providing for our family when you became my husband and I respect you. I promise not to undermine your authority or try to manipulate you to get my way.

As I mentioned before, all of my gifts and talents are for you. My viewpoint and feedback can benefit you when making decisions concerning our family, our businesses, or anything else. As your wife, I have been sent to help you and it means a lot to me when you accept my help. I want you and our children to be the first to benefit from the gifts God has placed within me so my desire is for us to operate as a partnership with you as the leader. Our agreement in matters concerning our family and our lives together is essential to accomplishing our goals.

> **Submitting to your leadership doesn't mean that I am inferior or incapable of leading. I am choosing to yield to you for our success as a couple.**

Accountability and Development

The thing about every great leader is that they are accountable to an even greater leader and continually submit to a process of development. Another way I know that I can trust your leadership is if I see you being accountable to other devoted husbands and being developed by someone with a proven track record of being a great leader and a faithful husband. Absence of accountability and development can quickly lead to stagnation or worse, the deterioration of our relationship.

Your Submission to God

I believe your submission to God is so key to your effectiveness as the leader of this family. As you seek God you receive the vision and instructions for our family so that we can stay within His perfect will. I understand that doesn't mean you will always get it right, but I know that if you continually submit to God we can get things back on track quickly.

> **Submission to God and developing our faith can help us grow together as a family.**

I feel so secure knowing that you pray concerning me and you regularly encourage me in my faith. I love that I can come to you for help with spiritual matters and I pray that we can always minister to each other in areas that need healing. I would like you to lead our family in regular prayer and devotion so that we can grow together and model for others and our children how to grow in relationship with God.

I know that as long as we are submitted to God above everything else, our marriage will be successful.

Let's Commit To:

1. **Accountability partners for our marriage and mentors for our individual ongoing spiritual development.**

2. **My submission to you and your submission to God for the leading of our family.**

3. **Pray for each other daily.**

Notes:

Dear Husbands,

I pray that within these pages you have discovered or rediscovered the world of love and support that is available with your wife when you two properly yield to each other in love. I hope you will use the material within these pages to have meaningful discussions with your wife and find out the unique ways you can better lead and serve your family.

For additional support, please check out the resources listed in the following pages or email info@rachelrenee.live with your questions. I am available to speak at women's and couples groups. For booking, please email info@RachelRenee.Live.

Dear Wives,

I pray that you have seen yourself in these pages as a woman who seeks to support and uplift her husband, yielding to his leadership while using your own strength and abilities to enhance and complement his. If you found some of the material challenging or disagree, that is to be expected. No two women are exactly the same, so please use this book as a resource to help you start a dialogue with your husband about your specific needs as his wife.

I do have resources specifically designed to support wives, available at www.EmpoweredWives.Club. Please connect with me there or at www.RachelRenee.Live. I am available to speak at women's and couples groups. For booking, please email info@RachelRenee.Live.

To My Husband,

I have been praying for you every day since July 18, 2016, which was shortly after I began writing this book. I am excited for the day that we are revealed to each other because there are so many wonderful things in store for us. I know God has had us both on a path of deep healing in preparation for each other and for worldwide ministry. I know that we are perfectly paired for each other's anointing, businesses, and ministries. I also know that our destinies are intertwined and that we will do major things together for the Kingdom of God.

You are a man of great purpose and vision and I am excited to be your helpmeet and partner in the amazing life God has planned for us.

I decree longevity, passion, Godliness, fruitfulness, unity, abundance, divine health, prosperity, fun, power, and above all, Love for our marriage for as long as we live.

All my Love,

MORE RESOURCES

Couples Academy: Hasani and Danielle Pettiford. www.couplesacademy.org

Empowered Wives Club: Rachel Renee. www.EmpoweredWives.Club

Praying While Waiting for Him/Praying While Waiting for Her: Zari Banks. www.ZariBanks.co

Preparing to Date Your Soulmate/Marriage: 21 Years of Doing it Wrong, 21 Days to Make it Right: Winston Tyrone Jackson, Sr.

The Blueprint: David A. Burrus. https://www.facebook.com/danthonyburrus

The Plural Thing/Love Better Manual/Love Better Institute: Linda Dominique Grosvenor-Holland. http://lovebetterinstitute.com

ABOUT THE AUTHOR

Rachel Renee, MBA is committed to empowering people to discover their power, passion, and purpose, freeing them to enjoy their lives and have fruitful relationships. She is also a publisher who has assisted many aspiring authors in realizing their dreams. Rachel has written and published seven books to date, including two devotionals: *The Rain Won't Hide These Tears* and *While the Sun Still Shines*, an anthology, *Bag Ladies: Unpacked*, and two Amazon bestsellers, *The Relationship Factor*, and *What's Your Story* along with the *What's Your Story Workbook*, which is a tool to assist aspiring authors in their writing process and the foundation of Rachel's programs for writers. *Dear Husband* is Rachel's newest title, launched for the purpose of supporting good marriages.

To learn more about Rachel's speaking, ghostwriting, coaching, or publishing services, please visit her website, www.RachelRenee.Live, contact her at info@RachelRenee.Live or call 919.375.8555. If you have enjoyed this book, please leave a review online at your favorite retailer's website.

Additional copies of this book can be ordered at
www.rainpublishing.com

www.ingramcontent.com/pod-product-compliance
Lightning Source LLC
Chambersburg PA
CBHW070551300426
44113CB00011B/1872